The Power of Habits

By James Nugent

Forward

I spent 22 years of my life in part time private practice as a counselor. The entire time I was amazed at how really smart people would make really poor choices over and over. One definition of crazy is when we do the same thing repeatedly and persist in the hope that something new will be the outcome. However, the people I was working with were not crazy (psychotic), just miserable. The wonderful people, with which I worked, were not unlike any of us. They were people who lived and loved and dreamed and deserved respect. Yet they destroyed the joy in their lives through habits of thoughts, feeling and behavior. This booklet is for those of us who dare to change their ways of using autopilot (habits), and squeeze even more joy and productivity out of life.

Disclaimer

This booklet is to be used for the purpose discussion only. It in no way is a substitute for competent psychological or spiritual counseling. No liability is implied or accepted.

Introduction

Habits rule are lives. How we think, feel, and behave are generally "on autopilot."

A Point of Theological

Many Doctors of the Catholic Church have taught that when we die, all that is left is our soul. The soul is a unique collection of our habits, our personality. These wise people advise serious consideration and action be applied to our habits which will be with us for eternity.

Be that as it may, our habits also affect the quality of our lives now.

The Good Things about Habits

Our habits serve us in almost every aspect of our lives. If we had to make an individual choice for each and every action we take in the morning; few of us would ever make to our jobs. Habits are a kind of autopilot. We give little or no thought to these habits and yet somehow we get out of bed and do all the preparatory tasks that we need to do in order the show up to work appropriately groomed. It is somewhat amazing that we accomplish most of these tasks while we are only half awake!

Let us take a little closer look at my typical morning. At 6:00 a.m. my alarm goes off. I have chosen a peaceful chime because I don't want to start my day on a painful or negative note. I have chosen the sound of birds making music. I put on some sandals and stagger outside to my rain gauge and note if there is any precipitation. I will report the results via the internet to CoCoRahs.org later in the morning.

By 6:05 am I am sitting on my stationary bicycle and sleepily workout until 6:35 am. During the last 10 minutes of my ride I pray the Psalter. This is the formal prayer, of the Roman

Catholic Church. I will pray the Psalter morning, evening and night.

So at 6:35 am I am ready to do the rest of my morning hygiene and get dressed for the day. All of this is done during various states of consciousness and with little actual intention. The actual choice to make this my routine was made years ago. Nowadays these habits serve me reliably.

However, habits do not just serve me in the groggy beginnings of my mornings. Rather they are with me throughout the day. There are at least 3 kinds of habits. There are habits of: thinking, feeling and behavior.

Habits of thinking

What we think about has a major impact on how we feel and act. For example, if I think about the world as a hostile place; I will feel like I have enemies around me. If I think of the world as a good place; I will feel that somehow in the end a good God will take care of me. I will feel much more relaxed and consoled.

It turns out that recent brain research has proven that our emotions reflect both real experiences and imagined experiences in much the same way. When people are put in a brain scanner and told to imagine being with the one they love; they have the exact same neural path ways stimulated as if they were with the object of their affection. This makes perfect sense but numerous schools of psychology and most of secular society rejects this simple idea. For if we can control our subjective emotional experiences; we are actually ultimately responsible for how we react (emotionally) to the world.

It seems easier to blame our responses on external forces. For example, I would actually be responsible for my own angry outbursts or laziness.

Accepting control of my habits of thought has been twisted by society into blaming oneself for one's problems. People worry that I am trying to shame or guilt them. I say, "Who said anything about guilt or shaming?" I am just pointing out that we are ultimately responsible for our habits of thought. Because we are responsible, we can change any thought that does not serve us well!

The way we think also has a major influence on how we behave. For example given enough angry thoughts and time most people will end up letting out that anger on somebody. We see the phenomena frequently in abused children. Because it is too dangerous to attack the abuser; little boys (or girls) will be mean to smaller children or pets. Teaching them empathy will do little to help. If you teach them that they are hurting somebody, they will just say, "Good I wanted to hurt them." I believe this is why 70% of sexually abused children will go on the abuse as adults if left untreated. The proper intervention is to help the child express their anger and hurt toward the offending parent. Interestingly one method of treatment starts out with a sand box and play therapy. The kids begin to act out in fantasy their hurts and what they would like to do to their abusers.

Most of us don't suffer from the extremes of abuse but we do suffer from things we have never given much thought. We suffer from our habits. For example young and old couples occasionally annoy one another. How they think, feel, and act will in the end effect the success and maintenance of the marriage.

I have been amazed in that when a married couple do anything together, they actually bring to the table every experience from their past too. The past experiences form by default their habits of thinking at the present.

One of the easiest illustrations will be seen in their sexual behavior. The wife and husband bring to the wedding bed every sex partner they have ever had. If there are many unhappy relationships in the wife's past she may actually bring suspicion and hurt feelings to the night of marital bliss. If the husband brings a dozen thoughtless and cavalier sexual encounters to honeymoon; he may bring the expectation that intimate relationships don't actually last forever.

Since both husband and wife bring these thoughts on "autopilot" they won't be aware of the potential disaster with which they are about to engage.

Thoughts lead to feelings. The feelings may be happy and excited on the surface but just below is the habitual way they have been feeling all these years. It is any surprise to anyone that women have trouble achieving orgasm and men have erectile dysfunction?

Feelings lead to behavior. So fumbling in the dark our newly paired married couple will go through the motions of making love while defensive, angry, hurt, and depressed. Fifty percent of the time, the couple will divorce. One of the leading causes of the breakups is sex. They will blame each other. They really didn't stand a chance because of their habitual ways of thinking, feeling, and acting.

This is not a book about the why couples fail to build strong healthy relationships. This is a book about how we can build good positive habits.

Building Good Habits

1. Sometimes good habits require big changes.

There are people and things that just suck the joy out of life. If you don't want to jettison them from your life, then you must think about them differently.

For example, in a Catholic marriage we marry for life. My job is to minister to my wife's physical, emotion, and spiritual needs. Her job is the same. If my wife is unloving to me, I just must work all the more diligently to heal her of her hurts and assist her in being her best possible person. Her job is the same.

Sometimes it might be difficult but then I remember that my joy comes from loving and assisting her. Her joy comes from the same place (guided by Christ). No one, is perfectly loving on earth; so all of a sudden everything is really all right. In fact, life, love, and marriage are great! How you think about things, affects everything else.

I am not suggesting that you must be Catholic to be happily married. I am suggesting that you must look at the inevitable conflicts that arise when two independent adults decide to spend their live together. It is critical that you find a way to habitually look at your spouse the will get you through the difficult times.

When I was in private practice I rarely accepted couples for counseling. There was usually little for me to work within a sad broken relationship. They almost always wanted to be able to say that they even tried counseling! They almost never wanted to give to other person. The relationships were built on "how much can I have." Any suggestion that, they were not giving enough usually resulted in an end to counseling. I was mostly unsuccessful in teaching people to work toward assisting their spouse in becoming the best person he/she could be. I stopped doing any couples counseling ten years before I retired.

2. Sometimes new habits require tiny changes.

If what you are doing in any relationship is not working; try something new. For example, if you are depressed at work because of your (butt head) boss; change your negative nickname you have given him. Smile at him and make an effort to be friendly. He might change just enough to make life palatable or at least you will feel a little better. Face it, it feels better to work for Kevin instead of butthead.

3. It takes time.

Somebody told me it takes 28 days to make a new habit. In my experience it seems like it takes 40 days. However, when I put my mind to it, I can make new habits.

4. Things that help make new habits of thinking, feeling and behaving.

I program myself by a bunch of techniques and I will just make a big list. Use anything that helps you and ignore the rest. Some things work better at different times.

-Make a mantra and say it often.

-Leave little reminders around. I like notes on the bathroom mirror and in my wallet. Make it a positive statement. Don't say, "I'm not fat." Say, "I'm becoming lean and healthy."

-Tell other supportive people.

-Celebrate wins.

-Never give up.

-Believe in the power to direct your life.

-Start with little habits before you try to take on big ones.

- Remember no one is perfect.

-If all else fails, pray.

-Pray first.

-Laughter is great medicine for changing your attitude.

-Attitude is really the only thing you can control.

-Pick how you want to feel and behave accordingly.

-Use meditation to affirm your positive habits.

-Exercise daily to get a dose of good feeling chemicals (endorphins) from your brain.

Hazards of Not Seizing Control of Your Habits

Like the small boat I anchored in my lagoon in front of my house. A bad habit is relentless and ultimately destructive. It is just like the small leaks in the boat which was a gift from a friend. She said it had small leaks, but not to worry about it.

I anchored the boat in about 12' of water and hung an anchor light on it.

The next morning I went to work, noting that the boat was fine. When I returned that evening it was underwater at the bottom of the lagoon! I waited until low tide and bailed it out. Sure enough it floated and then eventually sank by the next evening. The only thing had to do was wait until low tide, identify the holes, and fix them with underwater compound. It occurred to me that a leak in a boat was like a bad habit of mind, emotion or body. Sooner or later it will lead to disaster.

Also like a leak in a boat, bad habits never stop taking the joy out of life until you fix it. You can deny it is a problem like my friend did, but in the end it will be obvious.

Healthy and Happy Living

Believe it or not change can be very unnerving. Even good changes can feel weird. It is a major contrast from which you are accustomed. I have purposely built a good habit of relaxing when I am making a major change of habit in my life. If you don't look forward to, and enjoy change in your life it is unlikely that you will drop a bad habit and start a good habit. Just look at how many people fail to stop smoking or lose weight every January when it is time to make a New Year Resolution.

To make a major change in habit, you must program your mind until it almost becomes an obsession. You must want the change in habit so much that you will accept the temporary discomfort and anxiety of making the change. After a short while it will get easier!

Some people will complain all the time about their bad habits but never make the change.

I have had a friend since middle school (40 years). She is a bright and happy free spirited gal. Presently she is a high paid consultant which a major technology firm. Her one

consistent problem habit, all her life, has been picking dysfunctional men who cannot possibly ever be an equal partner. I have suggested over the years that she attend counseling. The few times she has, the counselor tried to fix the relationship instead of her.

She married two mentally ill men, and lived with a third. She also picked a homeless man, and later, a homeless women, as significant others. All five of these relationships were doomed from the start. However she will not see it as her responsibility to make sure that her partners are her equal or at least her equivalent. Every time she even gets close to a different kind of person (a healthy person), she get uncomfortable and bored.

So her life has been filled with endless strife, domestic violence, and unhappiness.

When I tried to point this out to her she was so offended that she said she would never talk to me again. However, I knew that she thrived off strife, so she was back to talking to me a month later. I have remove identifying features from the short summary of her life but I hope that she reads this and take it to heart. I hope that she will someday take the bull by the horns and build good habits in picking people for her relationships.

Patterns I have noticed in myself.

-Sometimes I try to change habits too quickly.

-Sometimes I try to change habits too slowly.

-Sometimes I blame myself.

-Sometimes I blame other people.

-Sometimes I forget that guilt is only good for telling me that something is wrong. Beyond that it is pathology.

-Sometimes I forget that life is a joyful adventure full of challenges and changes.

-Sometimes I forget that in my view of the universe there is a good God who loves us just the way we are, and wants us to be happy and well.

A Case for God

I think that belief (faith) in God can remedy most of our ills. Since believing is just a choice, and can immediately change how we think, feel and act; I suspect that we should adopt a religious attitude.

A universe with a good loving and forgiving God makes for an easier life. Don't get me wrong life can be filled with pain and hardships but having God in the back of your head can really help. Even Alcoholic Anonymous starts their 12 step program with the ideas that they have been unable to stop the drinking habit and the have decided to turn it over to a higher power.

Substance Abuse and Living Clean

Substance abuse is a complex habit and often needs medical and psychological/sociological Intervention. If you can't beat this kind of habit get help. It is confidential and often works. It saves lives. Maintaining a clean and sober life style takes a total commitment and the penalty for failure is often death. Take this kind of habit seriously and get help.

Habits can assist us in our goals.

Examples

-My habit of a morning workout before I really wake up, is a great way to get a little exercise and burn a few calories.

-My habit of reading the Psalter before I start the day puts my mind in a peaceful frame as I wake up. Having a peaceful mind set makes me be less likely to be angry and make mistakes when dealing with other people. Reading in the evening reminds me to let stuff go. Reading at bedtime actual allows me to dream all night peacefully.

-The habit of giving my wife a goodbye kiss every morning reminds me to always love, respect, support and assist her until death does us part.

-The habit of referring to my work as bringing gifts of wellness and health to humanity, helps me keep it all in perspective.

-The habit of enjoying the process of changing habits gives me the freedom to choose what I will without undo anxiety.

I wrote these words in 1979

We are what we are

We choose what we choose

We are nothing less and nothing more

Than what we choose to be

Best Regards

James Nugent

Olympia WA

12-27-14

Books by James Nugent

The Power of Habits

The Beginning School Counselor

Learning My Limits in Small Craft Boating

Eight Things You Need to Survive

Writing My First Books

How I Sailed From Olympia to the San Juan Islands, and Returned Safely

An Alternative Boating Guide to Southern Puget Sound

How and Why I lived Aboard

Kayaking Budd Inlet in South Puget Sound

Night Kayaking

Writing E-books and Making the Perfect Book

I Speak Esperanto

The Rainbow Road and Other Signs of God's Love

Living an Abundant Life, Within Your Means

Social Jujitsu and Powerful Principles for Managing Social Conflict

Blackjack on My Small Budget

A Little Benedictine Oblate Manuel

Without Speech

All things work

Loving Time with Your Creator

Personal Adventures in a Life of Learning

The Good News about Being Catholic

E-book Writing and Overcoming Barriers to Creativity

E-book Writing and Organizing Your Ideas

My Forty Days for Life 2013

Lifestyle Reality Observing

How to Sail in the Winter

How to Get Your Kid to Move Out

How to Get What Want

Sex, Abstinence, and Happiness

Cynthia Says Radio Show – Anger is a choice

More Good News about Being Catholic

The Solo Kayak

A Beach Naturalist on Southern Puget Sound

Clean House Clean Life

The Total Catholic Christian

Happiness is a Choice

Solo Kayak II

The Extraordinary Eucharistic Visitor

The Catholic Way of Dying

Available at Amazon.com in Kindle E-Book and or Audible Book or Paperback